The Mini Baker Cookbook

The Mini Baker Cookbook

Lars D. H. Hedbor & Jennifer Mendenhall

Copyright ©2014, All rights reserved. No part of this publication may reproduced, stored in a retrieval system, or transmitted in any form or by any means, electronic, mechanical, photocopy, or otherwise, without the prior expressed written permission of the publisher.

Printed in the United States.

Nutritional analyses are advisory only, and the actual nutritional values of the recipes as prepared will vary. All analyses are provided for the entire recipe, so if you determine that a portion size varies from the whole recipe, you should adjust the values accordingly.

We'd like to offer grateful acknowledgement of the staff at Sierra Pacific Crafts who supported and encouraged us in this endeavor. A special thank you to Beatrice McNew for last-minute copyediting, moral support and ceaseless encouragement.

Cover, illustrations, and book design: Lars D. H. Hedbor, Jennifer Mendenhall
Author photograph: Cassandra Sasse

First SPC Edition published 2014

ISBN 978-1-942319-00-9

Table of Contents

Desserts..1

Breakfasts...14

Sides & Appetizers.......28

Main Courses....................41

Index..53

Desserts

Life is uncertain. Always eat dessert first.
*   -John-Pierre Mallett*

Chocolate Pot de Crème

Ingredients for each mini baker

1/3 c	(75 ml)	heavy cream
1/3 c	(75 ml)	milk
½ t	(2 ml)	vanilla extract
1 T	(15 ml)	sugar
2 oz	(55 g)	dark chocolate, grated or chopped
2	regular	egg yolks, lightly beaten

Instructions

Preheat oven to 325° F (165° C).

Chop or grate chocolate into a bowl. Blend cream, milk, vanilla, and sugar in a small saucepan.

Heat until steaming, but not yet boiling, and then pour over chocolate, and whisk until the chocolate is melted and combined with the milk mixture.

Whisk the egg yolks slowly into the milk and chocolate mixture.

Strain into your mini baker, then put the mini baker in a baking dish, and set the baking dish in the oven.

Fill the baking dish with enough hot water to come half way up the side of the mini baker.

Bake for 20-30 minutes, until set, chill, and share it with someone special over candlelight with whipped cream. (*n.b.*: **You** are someone special.)

754 cal • 55g fat • 52g carb • 2g fiber • 14g protein

Pumpkin Custard

Ingredients for each mini baker

½ c	(120 ml)	pumpkin, canned
1 T	(15 ml)	egg substitute/lightly beaten egg
¼ c	(60 ml)	evaporated milk
2 T	(30 ml)	sugar
	pinch	cinnamon
	pinch	ground ginger
	pinch	ground cloves

Instructions

Preheat oven to 350° F (180° C). Grease mini baker well.

Blend all ingredients together well, and transfer to the mini baker.

Bake for 45 minutes to an hour, and serve warm, topped with whipped cream.

230 cal • 5g fat • 42g carb • 4g fiber • 8g protein

Desserts

Caramel Custard

Ingredients for each mini baker

1	large	egg
2/3 c	(150 ml)	milk
4 T	(60 ml)	sugar
¼ t	(1 ml)	vanilla extract
2 T	(30 ml)	sugar
2 t	(10 ml)	water
2 t	(10 ml)	salted butter

Instructions

Preheat oven to 350° F (180° C).

Blend egg, milk, sugar, and vanilla together, and strain into your mini baker.

Place the mini baker into a baking dish, and put it in the oven. Fill the baking dish with enough boiling water to come halfway up the side of the mini baker, then bake for 35-40 minutes or until a knife inserted in the center comes out clean.

When the custard comes out of the oven, cool it completely.

Meanwhile, mix the sugar and water in a microwave-safe bowl or cup, and microwave on high for approximately 90 seconds, watching carefully for when it first starts to turn brown.

Very carefully mix the butter into the hot sugar mix—it may spatter—and continue blending until it is a smooth.

Immediately pour the caramel over the custard. Let cool, even overnight if you like, and serve with a dollop of whipped cream. If you're making this to split with someone you love, make two instead.

494 cal • 16g fat • 81g carb • 0g fiber • 11g protein

Lemon Puff Pudding

Ingredients for each mini baker

1	large	egg, separated
	pinch	salt
5 T	(75 ml)	sugar, divided
1 T	(15 ml)	butter, softened
4 t	(20 ml)	flour
½ t	(2 ml)	lemon rind, grated
4 t	(20 ml)	lemon juice
½ c	(120 ml)	milk

Instructions

Preheat oven to 325° F (165° C), butter your mini baker.

Beat egg white and salt together until stiff peaks form. Add 2 T (30 ml) sugar and stir to combine, then set aside.

Cream together butter, remaining 3 T (45 ml) sugar, and flour. Add egg yolk and beat well. Stir in the lemon juice and milk.

Gently fold in the egg white mixture, and then transfer to your mini baker.

Place mini baker in a baking dish, put in the oven, and fill the baking dish with hot water about halfway up the side of the mini baker. Bake for 35-40 minutes, until browned, and serve warm with good strong Swedish coffee.

508 cal • 19g fat • 76g carb • 0g fiber • 12g protein

Yogurt Soufflé

Ingredients for each mini baker

1/3 c	(75 ml)	Greek yogurt
1	large	egg, separated
1 T	(15 ml)	flour
	dash	vanilla extract
	pinch	salt
2 t	(10 ml)	sugar

Don't let the word "soufflé" scare you—whether you serve this right out of the oven while it is risen high above the sides of the dish, or after it has cooled and settled back down (or if it never rises), it will be light and fluffy and delicious. All "failure" should be so great!

Instructions

Preheat oven to 375° F (190° C). Butter your mini baker, then put some sugar in it and tilt it about to coat the inside; pour out the excess sugar.

Whisk together the yogurt, egg yolk, flour, sugar, salt, and vanilla.

Separately, beat the egg white and sugar until soft peaks form. Gradually fold together with the yogurt mixture, and then transfer to the mini baker.

Place the mini baker on a baking sheet, and bake for 15 minutes, until the soufflé rises evenly and is lightly browned around the edges. If at all possible, check it without opening the oven.

Serve immediately, or allow to "fall" and serve cooled.

207 cal • 7g fat • 19g carb • 0g fiber • 17g protein

Gingerbread Soufflé

Ingredients for each mini baker

2 T	(30 ml)	milk
4 t	(20 ml)	sugar
2 t	(10 ml)	flour
	pinch	salt
1 T	(15 ml)	molasses
1 t	(5 ml)	butter, softened
	pinch	ground cloves
	pinch	cinnamon
	pinch	powdered ginger
¼ t	(2 ml)	vanilla extract
1	large	egg, separated

Instructions

Preheat oven to 350° F (175° C). Butter your mini baker and pour in sugar, tipping to coat the inside of the mini baker, and then pour out the excess.

In a microwave-safe cup, whisk together the milk, sugar, flour, and salt until smooth. Microwave for 30 seconds, or until it comes to a boil.

Immediately add the molasses, butter, cloves, cinnamon, ginger, and vanilla. Let cool a bit, and then beat in the egg yolk.

Beat the egg white until stiff peaks form, and then fold into the milk mixture a third at a time, until well blended.

Spoon batter into your mini baker, place it on a cookie sheet, and bake for 25 minutes, or until puffed and set. Serve immediately with whipped cream.

267 cal • 10g fat • 38g carb • 0g fiber • 8g protein

Chocolate Lava Cake

Ingredients for each mini baker

2 T	(30 ml)	butter
2 oz	(55 g)	dark chocolate
1	large	egg
1	large	egg yolk
2 T	(30 ml)	sugar
2 T	(30 ml)	flour
1 t	(5 ml)	cocoa powder
	pinch	salt

This is a purely decadent end to any meal, and it is surprisingly easy to put together.

Instructions

Put the butter and chocolate in the mini baker and microwave for 45-60 seconds, or until mostly melted. Remove and blend together until smooth.

In a small bowl, whisk together egg, egg yolk, and sugar for about 3 minutes, until the mixture is pale yellow and all of the sugar has dissolved.

Pour into the chocolate mixture, and whisk until well blended.

Sift together the flour, cocoa powder, and salt, then fold into the chocolate and egg mixture gently with a small spatula.

Start the oven preheating to 425° F (220° C). Refrigerate mini baker for 30 minutes, then put into a shallow baking dish, place in the oven, and fill the baking dish with water until it is halfway up the side of the mini baker.

Bake for 25 minutes, or until set and slightly browned, then serve warm with a sprinkle of powdered sugar over the top.

778 cal • 49g fat • 71g carb • 3g fiber • 15g protein

Blackberry Cobbler

Ingredients for each mini baker

1 T	(15 ml)	butter
1/3 c	(75 ml)	flour
1/3 c	(75 ml)	sugar
¼ t	(1 ml)	baking powder
pinch		salt
3 T	(45 ml)	milk
½ c	(120 ml)	blackberries, fresh or frozen (or substitute any fruit you like)

Instructions

Preheat oven to 325° F (165° C).

Melt butter in the mini baker in the microwave.

Sift together flour, sugar, baking powder, and salt. Stir in milk and blend thoroughly.

Pour over butter in mini baker and drop the blackberries on top of the batter.

Bake for 30 minutes, or until golden brown; fruit will settle down to the bottom. Serve warm, with ice cream.

531 cal • 13g fat • 101g carb • 5g fiber • 7g protein

Desserts

Blueberry Crumble

Ingredients for each mini baker

¼ c	(60 ml)	apple, peeled & diced
½ c	(120 ml)	blueberries
½ t	(2 ml)	sugar
¼ t	(1 ml)	cinnamon
½ T	(7 ml)	flour
1 T	(15 ml)	flour
2 T	(30 ml)	brown sugar
1 T	(15 ml)	butter
	pinch	cinnamon
2 T	(30 ml)	rolled oats

Instructions

Preheat oven to 350° F (175° C), and grease your mini baker.

Mix the apple, blueberries, sugar, cinnamon, and flour. Transfer the fruit mixture to your mini baker.

Combine the flour and brown sugar. Blend in the butter, using a fork or your fingers until the mixture resembles coarse crumbs. Add the cinnamon and the oats and mix well.

Sprinkle the topping over the fruit mixture, place on a cookie sheet, and bake for 35-40 minutes, or until the fruit is tender. Serve warm with ice cream.

640 cal • 25g fat • 102g carb • 9g fiber • 7g protein

Pumpkin-Pear Crisp

Ingredients for each mini baker

1/3 c	(75 ml)	sugar pumpkin flesh, cubed
2 t	(10 ml)	maple syrup
1 t	(5 ml)	lemon juice
½ t	(2 ml)	brown sugar
¼ t	(1 ml)	cinnamon
pinch		ground cloves
dash		vanilla extract
2/3 c	(150 ml)	pear, peeled, cored, & cubed
1 T	(15 ml)	rolled oats
1 T	(15 ml)	pumpkin seeds (pepitas)
1 T	(15 ml)	brown sugar
1 T	(15 ml)	butter, softened
pinch		cinnamon

Instructions

Preheat oven to 375° F (190° C) and grease your mini bakers.

Put ¼ c water in a small saucepan. Add pumpkin, syrup, lemon juice, brown sugar, cinnamon, and cloves, and bring them to a simmer over medium heat.

Cook for about 7 minutes, or until pumpkin is just tender, and then add the vanilla and pears and cook for another 10 minutes. Transfer to the mini baker.

Mix together oats, pepitas, brown sugar, butter, and cinnamon, blending until the butter is well combined.

Sprinkle over the fruit, and then bake for 25-30 minutes, until the filling is bubbling at the edges. Let cool a bit before serving with vanilla ice cream.

318 cal • 16g fat • 44g carb • 5g fiber • 4g protein

Chocolate Chip Cookie

Ingredients for each mini baker

1 T	(15 ml)	butter
1 T	(15 ml)	sugar
1 T	(15 ml)	brown sugar
	dash	vanilla extract
	pinch	salt
1	large	egg yolk
¼ c	(60 ml)	flour
2 T	(30 ml)	chocolate chips

Instructions

Put butter in mini baker and microwave on high for about 20-30 seconds, until melted. Whisk in sugars, vanilla, salt, and egg yolk. Blend in flour until smooth, and then mix in the chocolate chips.

Microwave on high for 40-60 seconds, until set, and serve immediately with milk.

468 cal • 23g fat • 59g carb • 2g fiber • 8g protein

Monkey Bread

Ingredients for each mini baker

½ c	(120 ml)	flour
½ T	(7 ml)	sugar
¼ t	(1 ml)	salt
¼ t	(1 ml)	yeast
1 T	(15 ml)	oil
3 T	(45 ml)	water
1 T	(15 ml)	butter
3 T	(45 ml)	sugar
½ T	(7 ml)	cinnamon

Instructions

Blend the flour, sugar, salt, and yeast together in a small bowl. Add the oil and the water, and stir with a stout wooden spoon until it forms a ball. (There may be some remaining flour in the bowl at this stage.)

Turn the dough and any remaining flour out onto a floured board, and knead together for about five minutes, until all of the flour is incorporated, and the dough is smooth and elastic. If the dough is still sticky to the touch, add a dusting of flour and continue kneading; if it is dry or won't absorb the remaining flour, sprinkle some water over it and continue kneading. Lightly oil your mini baker, put the dough in it, and put the lid on. Leave the dough to rise for an hour or so, until it doubles in volume.

Melt the butter in a small bowl, and mix the sugar and cinnamon together in another bowl. Lightly flour your kneading surface again, and turn the dough out onto it. Knead briefly, and then pinch off marble-size pieces of dough, rolling them between your hands to make them into balls. Dip each ball in the butter, then roll it in the cinnamon sugar, and put each into the mini baker. Put the lid back on, and put it in a warm place to rise again to double its volume.

Meanwhile, preheat oven to 425° F (220° C). When the dough has risen, put the mini baker in the oven, bake for 10 minutes, reduce heat to 350° F (175° C), and bake for another 30 minutes, or until golden brown.

624 cal • 26g fat • 94g carb • 4g fiber • 7g protein

Cannoli Dip

Ingredients for each mini baker

½ c	(120 ml)	ricotta cheese
2 oz	(55 g)	cream cheese
6 T	(90 ml)	confectioners' sugar
¼ t	(1 ml)	vanilla extract
¼ c	(60 ml)	mini chocolate chips

Instructions

In a small bowl, beat ricotta cheese and cream cheese together until smooth. Add sugar and vanilla, and stir until completely combined.

Fold in chocolate chips and transfer to your mini baker. Cover with lid for at least 10 minutes, or overnight to let the flavors meld.

Top with a sprinkling of additional chocolate chips. Serve with graham crackers, pizzelles, or broken-up waffle cones.

808 cal • 45g fat • 79g carb • 1g fiber • 23g protein

Breakfasts

Sometimes I believe in as many as six impossible things before breakfast.
- Alice in Wonderland

Spanish Egg Cup

Ingredients for each mini baker

¼ lb	(115 g)	potatoes, peeled and cubed
¼ c	(60 ml)	red onion, diced
¼ c	(60 ml)	bell pepper, seeded and diced
¼ c	(60 ml)	tomato, diced
2 t	(10 ml)	minced garlic
2 T	(30 ml)	black olives, coarsely chopped
¼ c	(60 ml)	chorizo sausage, broken up

- or -

1-2	slices	bacon, cut into small pieces
1	large	egg
		smoked paprika
		black pepper

Instructions

Preheat oven to 375° F (185° C). Put a pot of lightly-salted water on to boil. Prepare ingredients.

Put the potatoes in the boiling water, and cook for 10 minutes, until just tender.

Meanwhile fry sausage or bacon in a skillet. Remove bacon or sausage from the skillet and put on paper towel to drain.

Add just enough olive oil to the skillet to prevent sticking, then sauté the onion for 2 minutes, then add the bell pepper and cook for another 3 minutes. Add tomato and garlic, and cook over low heat for another 10 minutes.

Drain potatoes and add to onion mixture, together with olives. Season with paprika and pepper.

Transfer mixture to mini baker and crumble the bacon or sausage over it. Make a well in the center with a spoon, and crack egg into it.

Bake for 10-12 minutes, until the eggs are set, and serve hot with a good crusty bread and coffee.

309 cal • 16g fat • 27g carb • 5g fiber • 15g protein

Caprese Baked Eggs

Ingredients for each mini baker

½ c	(120 ml)	grape tomatoes, halved
½ c	(120 ml)	mozzarella cheese, cubed
4-5	leaves	fresh basil, coarsely chopped
1 T	(15 ml)	cream or milk
2	large	eggs

Bursting with flavor, this breakfast will transport you to a sunny morning on the Mediterranean, listening to the breezes play through the branches of olive trees that were old when Caesar played beneath them.

Instructions

Preheat oven to 350° F (175° C). Prepare ingredients.

Put about half of the cheese, tomatoes, and basil into your mini baker, pour the egg mixture over them, and top with the remainder.

Place the mini baker on a cookie sheet and bake for 8-10 minutes, then broil for about another 5 minutes, until your eggs are well set.

Serve immediately with a toasted slice of crusty Italian bread.

302 cal • 19g fat • 6g carb • 2g fiber • 28g protein

Bacon, Egg & Cheddar Bake

Ingredients for each mini baker

2	slices	bacon, cut into half length strips
2	large	eggs
1 t	(5 ml)	cream or milk
¼ c	(60 ml)	shredded cheddar cheese

Instructions

Preheat oven to 375° F (185° C).

Lay bacon in the bottom of your mini baker.

Microwave for 2-4 minutes, until the bacon is crisp and drain off the grease.

Whisk eggs and cream together until foamy, and pour over the bacon. Top with the cheese.

Bake for 10-12 minutes, until the eggs are set and the cheese is bubbly and melted. Serve hot with fresh fruit.

383 cal • 27g fat • 2g carb • 0g fiber • 32g protein

Breakfast Casserole

Ingredients for each mini baker

2	slices	Canadian bacon
½ c	(120 ml)	potato, peeled & shredded
2 T	(30 ml)	onion, chopped
2	large	eggs
1 T	(15 ml)	cream or milk

Instructions

Preheat oven to 375° F (185° C). Prepare ingredients and lightly grease your mini baker.

Layer a slice of the bacon, potatoes, and onion.

Blend eggs and cream or milk together, and then pour over the mixture. Top with the second slice of bacon.

Bake for 25-30 minutes, or until the eggs are well set, to give the potatoes time to cook through.

260 cal • 13g fat • 10g carb • 1g fiber • 24g protein

Scottish Oats

Ingredients for each mini baker

¼ c	(60 ml)	steel-cut oats
2 T	(30 ml)	brown sugar
1 t	(5 ml)	butter
¼ c	(60 ml)	milk
¾ c	(180 ml)	water
	dash	cinnamon
	dash	salt

Instructions

Preheat oven to 225° F (110° C).

Mix oats, sugar, cinnamon, and salt in your mini baker. Add butter, milk, and water.

Cover tightly with the lid, and place in the oven, with a cookie sheet beneath to catch any drips. Bake overnight (6-8 hours), stir well, and serve with hot coffee and fresh orange juice.

289 cal • 8g fat • 48g carb • 4g fiber • 7g protein

Blueberry Muffin

Ingredients for each mini baker

½ c	(120 ml)	flour
3 T	(45 ml)	sugar
½ t	(2 ml)	salt
½ t	(2 ml)	cinnamon
½ t	(2 ml)	baking powder
¼ c	(60 ml)	milk
2 t	(10 ml)	oil
½ c	(120 ml)	blueberries, fresh or frozen

Instructions

Preheat oven to 375° F (180° C). Grease your mini baker well.

Sift together flour, sugar, salt, cinnamon, and baking powder into a small bowl or measuring cup. Separately, blend together the milk and oil, then blend into the flour mixture.

Add the blueberries, stir, and pour into mini baker.

Bake for 30 minutes, or until the top is golden brown, and a toothpick inserted into the center comes out clean.

526 cal • 11g fat • 100g carb • 4g fiber • 9g protein

Breakfasts

Apple Bran Muffin

Ingredients for each mini baker

1/3 c	(75 ml)	oat bran
¼ c	(60 ml)	flour
¼ t	(1 ml)	baking powder
pinch		cinnamon
¼ c	(60 ml)	milk
1 T	(15 ml)	molasses
1 t	(5 ml)	oil
2 T	(30 ml)	applesauce
½ T	(7 ml)	egg substitute/lightly beaten egg
dash		vanilla extract
4 t	(20 ml)	pecans, chopped
¼ c	(60 ml)	apple, diced

Instructions

Preheat oven to 400° F (205° C) and grease your mini baker.

Blend bran, flour, baking powder, and cinnamon. In a separate bowl, blend milk, molasses, applesauce, oil, egg, and vanilla. Add, along with the raisins, pecans, and apple, to the flour mixture and stir until just moistened.

Pour into your mini baker and bake for 15-20 minutes, or until a toothpick inserted into the center comes out clean.

417 cal • 13g fat • 66g carb • 5g fiber • 11g protein

Lemon Poppyseed Muffin

Ingredients for each mini baker

2 T	(30 ml)	sugar
	pinch	lemon zest
1/3 c	(75 ml)	flour
½ t	(2 ml)	baking powder
	pinch	salt
1 t	(5 ml)	poppy seeds
2 T	(30 ml)	plain Greek yogurt
1 T	(15 ml)	egg substitute/lightly beaten egg
1 t	(5 ml)	lemon juice
¼ t	(1 ml)	vanilla extract
1 T	(15 ml)	butter, melted
2 T	(30 ml)	confectioners' sugar
½ t	(2 ml)	lemon juice

Instructions

Preheat oven to 400° F (205° C), and grease your mini baker.

Mix the sugar, lemon zest, flour, baking powder, salt, and poppy seeds together. Separately, blend the yogurt, egg, lemon juice, vanilla, and butter thoroughly.

Combine the wet and dry ingredients and stir just enough to blend.

Pour batter into your mini baker, and bake for 18-20 minutes, or until a toothpick inserted into the center comes out clean. Remove from the oven and set aside to cool.

Meanwhile, blend the confectioners' sugar and lemon juice to make the glaze; add more lemon juice if necessary, to reach a consistency where it drizzles readily from the tip of a spoon.

Drizzle glaze over the muffin, and serve with hot tea.

451 cal • 14g fat • 74g carb • 1g fiber • 9g protein

Breakfasts

French Toast Cup

Ingredients for each mini baker

1 T	(15 ml)	butter
¼ c	(60 ml)	milk
1	large	egg
½ t	(2 ml)	sugar
¼ t	(1 ml)	cinnamon
¼ t	(1 ml)	vanilla extract
	pinch	salt
1 c	(225 ml)	stale bread, cut into cubes

Instructions

Preheat oven to 350° F (175° C).

Melt the butter in your mini baker. Add the milk, egg, sugar, cinnamon, vanilla, and salt, and stir well.

Add the bread, and toss with a fork to cover well. Cover and chill for an hour or so to let the egg mixture soak into the bread.

Put in the oven and bake for 15-20 minutes, or until set. Serve with warm maple syrup or a dusting of powdered sugar.

303 cal • 19g fat • 22g carb • 1g fiber • 11g protein

German Pancake

Ingredients for each mini baker

1	large	egg
3 T	(45 ml)	milk
2 t	(10 ml)	butter, melted
3 T	(45 ml)	flour
¼ t	(1 ml)	vanilla extract
	pinch	salt

Instructions

Preheat oven to 400° F (205° C). Generously grease your mini baker.

Blend the egg, milk, butter, and vanilla together thoroughly. Add the flour and salt, and blend until there are no lumps.

Pour the batter into the mini baker, then bake for 15 minutes, or until puffed up and golden-brown.

Remove from the oven and wait for the pancake to deflate, then serve with honey or strawberry jam.

252 cal • 14g fat • 21g carb • 1g fiber • 10g protein

Coffee Cake

Ingredients for each mini baker

½ c	(120 ml)	flour
¼ c	(60 ml)	sugar
½ t	(2 ml)	baking powder
¼ t	(1 ml)	cinnamon
pinch		salt
2 T	(30 ml)	butter
¼ c	(60 ml)	milk

Streusel Topping:

¼ c	(60 ml)	oats
2 T	(30 ml)	brown sugar
¼ t	(1 ml)	cinnamon
1 T	(15 ml)	butter

Instructions

Preheat oven to 375° F (180° C). Grease the mini baker well.

Sift together the flour, sugar, baking powder, cinnamon, and salt. Blend in the butter, cutting it into the flour mixture until the mixture resembles a coarse meal. Stir in the milk, and pour into the mini baker.

Now, blend together the oats, brown sugar, cinnamon, and butter until it forms sticky clumps, and spread it over the top of the batter.

Bake for 45 minutes, or until a toothpick inserted into the center comes out clean.

904 cal • 38g fat • 134g carb • 4g fiber • 12g protein

Oven Pancake

Ingredients for each mini baker

1	large	egg
¼ c	(60 ml)	milk
1 T	(15 ml)	butter, melted
½ c	(120 ml)	flour
1 t	(5 ml)	baking powder
2 T	(30 ml)	sugar

Instructions

Preheat oven to 375° F (185° C).

Whisk together egg, milk, and butter.

Sift together remaining ingredients, and then blend into egg mixture until just smooth. Do not over mix, or it will be tough.

Pour into mini baker, and bake for about 30 minutes, or until a toothpick inserted into the top comes out clean.

Serve with butter and lots of syrup - it will absorb much more than an ordinary pancake!

529 cal • 18g fat • 77g carb • 2g fiber • 15g protein

Quiche Lorraine

Ingredients for each mini baker

10"	(25 cm)	diameter pie pastry
1	slice	bacon, fried crisp & crumbled
2 T	(30 ml)	onion, chopped finely
¼ c	(60 ml)	cheddar cheese, shredded
2	large	eggs
3 T	(45 ml)	cream
		nutmeg

Instructions

Preheat oven to 375° F (185° C).

Prepare pastry and press it into the bottom of the mini baker, trimming the excess off at the edge of the rim. Poke the crust all over with the tines of a fork, and bake for 7 minutes.

Meanwhile, for each quiche, prepare the bacon, onion, and cheese.

Whisk together the eggs and cream, with a dash of nutmeg.

When the pre-baked pastry has cooled a bit, sprinkle the cheese, onion, and bacon into the crust, and then pour the egg mixture over it.

Bake for 30-35 minutes, until well-set. Top with more shredded cheese just before removing from the oven, if you like. Serve warm or cold.

763 cal • 48g fat • 53g carb • 2g fiber • 30g protein

Sides & Appetizers

When baking, follow directions. When cooking, go by your own taste.
-Laiko Bahrs

Ham & Spinach Pasta

Ingredients for each mini baker

1/3 c	(75 ml)	uncooked penne pasta
2 oz	(55 g)	fresh baby spinach
1 t	(5 ml)	olive oil
¼ c	(60 ml)	onion, chopped
½ T	(7 ml)	flour
¼ t	(1 ml)	dry mustard
¼ t	(1 ml)	black pepper
¼ c	(60 ml)	milk
2 T	(30 ml)	mozzarella cheese, shredded
½ T	(7 ml)	parmesean cheese, shredded
1 oz	(25 g)	ham, cooked & cubed

Instructions

Preheat oven to 400° F (205° C).

Cook pasta according to package instructions. Wash spinach and put in a colander over the sink. When the pasta is done, pour it and its cooking water over the spinach and mix together to blanch the spinach. Set aside.

Sauteé the onion in the olive oil until softened, and then add in the flour, dry mustard, and pepper. Stir and cook for another minute.

Stir in the milk, and continue cooking until slightly thickened, then cook and stir for another minute.

Gradually add the cheeses, and stir until they are melted and well-blended into the sauce. Add the pasta mixture and ham, toss gently to cover, and transfer to the mini baker.

Bake for about 10 minutes, or until the top is just browning. Serve hot with a nice chianti.

416 cal • 17g fat • 43g carb • 2g fiber • 24g protein

Cheesy Broccoli

Ingredients for each mini baker

1 c	(225 ml)	broccoli florets, fresh or frozen
½ c	(120 ml)	milk
2 t	(10 ml)	flour
	pinch	white pepper
½ c	(60 ml)	cheddar cheese, shredded

Instructions

Preheat oven to 350° F (175° C).

Bring a small pot of water to a boil, and blanch the broccoli in it for about 3 minutes. Drain and transfer the broccoli to your mini baker.

Whisk together the milk, flour, and white pepper. Bring the mixture to a boil over medium-high heat, stirring constantly. Reduce heat, and cook until slightly thickened, continuing to stir constantly.

Stir in the cheese, and whisk until melted and well blended. Pour the cheese mixture over the broccoli. Top with a little more shredded cheese, if you like.

Bake for 15-20 minutes, or until the broccoli is tender and the cheese slightly browned.

225 cal • 12g fat • 16g carb • 2g fiber • 14g protein

Sides & Appetizers

Paprika Cauliflower

Ingredients for each mini baker

1½ c	(345 ml)	cauliflower, chopped
2 t	(10 ml)	olive oil
¼ t	(1 ml)	paprika, hot, sweet, or smoked

Instructions

Preheat oven to 350° F (175° C).

Toss the cauliflower, oil, and paprika together. Transfer to the mini baker, cover tightly with the lid and bake for 20-30 minutes, or until tender.

106 cal • 10g fat • 5g carb • 3g fiber • 2g protein

Scalloped Potatoes

Ingredients for each mini baker

1 c	(225 ml)	potatoes, peeled and sliced
½ c	(120 ml)	milk
2 T	(15 ml)	butter, softened
pinch		salt
pinch		white pepper

Instructions

Preheat oven to 350° F (175° C), and grease your mini baker.

Arrange potatoes in layers in the mini baker, and dot each layer with butter.

Blend the salt and pepper with the milk, and pour it over the potatoes.

Bake 30-40 min, until browned and the potatoes are tender; serve hot.

263 cal • 14g fat • 29g carb • 3.4g fiber • 7g protein

Sides & Appetizers

Candied Sweet Potatoes

Ingredients for each mini baker

1 c	(225 ml)	sweet potatoes, peeled and cubed
¼ c	(60 ml)	brown sugar
	dash	cinnamon
2 t	(10 ml)	butter
¼ c	(60 ml)	marshmallows

Instructions

Preheat oven to 375° F (190° C), and grease your mini baker.

Toss the sweet potatoes with the brown sugar and cinnamon to coat, and transfer to the mini baker. Dot with butter.

Bake for 30-40 minutes, or until the potatoes are tender. Top with marshmallows and broil until the marshmallows are golden brown.

466 cal • 8g fat • 98g carb • 6g fiber • 3g protein

Cheesy Garlic Mashed Potatoes

Ingredients for each mini baker

1½ c	(345 ml)	potatoes, peeled and cubed
2	cloves	garlic, sliced thickly
2 T	(30 ml)	milk
½ T	(7 ml)	butter
	pinch	white pepper
	pinch	salt
2 T	(30 ml)	Parmesean cheese, grated

Instructions

Preheat oven to 425° F (220° C).

Bring a small pot of water to a boil. Add potatoes and garlic, reduce heat, and simmer for 10 minutes, or until the potatoes are tender.

Drain, mash with a potato masher or the back of a wooden spoon, and then add milk, butter, white pepper, and salt. Stir well, adding more milk if necessary for a creamy texture.

Transfer to your mini baker, top with the Parmesean cheese, and bake for 20 minutes, or until the cheese is golden brown.

256 cal • 8g fat • 38g carb • 5g fiber • 8g protein

Sides & Appetizers

Dirty Rice

Ingredients for each mini baker

1 c	(180 ml)	white rice, cooked
2 oz	(55 g)	uncooked sausage or ground beef
1 T	(15 ml)	celery, chopped fine
1 T	(15 ml)	onion, minced
1 T	(15 ml)	bell pepper, diced
1 t	(5 ml)	garlic, minced
¼ t	(1 ml)	parsley
1 t	(5 ml)	creole seasoning blend

Instructions

Mix the meat and the celery, onion, bell pepper, and garlic. Put the mixture into your mini baker and microwave for 90 seconds, or until the meat is cooked through and the vegetables are tender.

Blend in the parsley and creole seasoning, and then add the rice and stir to mix thoroughly. Serve warm with a good Cajun hot sauce.

739 cal • 8g fat • 115g carb • 2g fiber • 45g protein

Buffalo Chicken Dip

Ingredients for each mini baker

2 oz	(60 g)	cream cheese, softened
2 T	(30 ml)	Buffalo hot sauce
2 T	(30 ml)	ranch dressing
½ c	(120 ml)	chicken meat, cooked & shredded
2 T	(30 ml)	blue cheese, crumbled

Instructions

Preheat oven to 350° F (175° C).

Combine all ingredients in your mini baker. Cover and bake for 20 minutes, or until heated through. Serve with celery and carrot sticks and hearty crackers.

413 cal • 31g fat • 4g carb • 0g fiber • 29g protein

Real Queso Salsa Dip

Ingredients for each mini baker

2 T	(30 ml)	beer
1½ t	(7 ml)	cornstarch
¼ c	(60 ml)	salsa
1 c	(225 ml)	sharp cheddar, grated

Instructions

Preheat oven to 300° F (150° C). Place mini baker in oven to warm.

In a small saucepan, whisk together beer and cornstarch until smooth. Blend in the salsa, and bring it to a simmer over medium heat. Stir in the cheese, a quarter at a time, until each portion is melted and combined. Add more cheese if you like.

Remove your mini baker from oven, transfer dip to the mini baker and serve immediately with tortillas and beer.

478 cal • 36g fat • 10g carb • 1g fiber • 28g protein

Sweet Onion Dip

Ingredients for each mini baker

½ c	(120 ml)	mayonnaise
2 T	(30 ml)	sour cream
2 T	(30 ml)	Swiss cheese, grated
2 T	(30 ml)	sharp cheddar cheese, grated
¾ c	(175 ml)	sweet onions, minced finely
pinch		garlic powder
2 T	(30 ml)	Swiss cheese, grated
2 T	(30 ml)	sharp cheddar cheese, grated

Use Walla Walla or Vidalia onions in this for the best flavor, or else sauteé your onions first to sweeten them.

Instructions

Preheat oven to 350° F (175° C), and grease your mini-baker.

In a small bowl, combine the mayonnaise, sour cream, the first portions of Swiss cheese and cheddar cheese, onions, and garlic powder. Transfer to the mini baker and top with the remaining cheese.

Bake for 30-40 minutes, or until the top is golden brown and bubbly. Serve with pita chips and Prosecco.

789 cal • 62g fat • 43g carb • 3g fiber • 17g protein

Bacon & Shallots Dip

Ingredients for each mini baker

2	slices	bacon, diced
2 T	(30 ml)	shallots, sliced thinly
2 oz	(60 g)	cream cheese
2 T	(30 ml)	mayonnaise
2 T	(30 ml)	sour cream
½ t	(2 ml)	Dijon mustard
½ t	(2 ml)	horseradish
½ c	(120 ml)	Swiss cheese, grated
1 t	(5 ml)	Parmesan cheese, grated

Instructions

Preheat oven to 400° F (205° C).

Cook bacon until crisp, remove from pan and drain thoroughly.

Add shallots to pan and sauteé over low heat for 5-10 minutes, or until soft and caramelized. Remove from pan and drain.

In a small bowl, blend cream cheese, mayonnaise, sour cream, mustard, and horseradish together thoroughly. Stir in the Swiss cheese, shallots, and bacon, and transfer to your mini baker. Top with Parmesan.

Bake for 20 minutes, or until the top is golden brown and bubbly. Serve with toasted slices of French bread.

684 cal • 57g fat • 17g carb • 0g fiber • 27g protein

Main Dishes

No one who cooks, cooks alone. Even at her most solitary, a cook in the kitchen is surrounded by generations of cooks past.
- Laurie Colwin

French Onion Soup

Ingredients for each mini baker

½	medium	onion, sliced thinly
1 T	(15 ml)	butter
½	clove	garlic, minced
½ T	(7ml)	flour
1 c	(225 ml)	beef broth
¼ c	(60 ml)	white wine
	pinch	dried thyme
1	slice	French bread, toasted
3 T	(45 ml)	Gruyere or Swiss cheese, shredded

Instructions

In a saucepan over medium heat, sauteé onions in butter until soft. Add flour and garlic, and continue sauteéing until the onions have caramelized to a rich, brown color.

Add broth, wine, and thyme, and simmer over low heat for about 30 minutes.

Transfer to mini baker, lay the bread on top of it, and sprinkle the cheese over the bread.

Broil on low until the cheese is melted and slightly browned, and serve hot.

406 cal • 20g fat • 29g carb • 2g fiber • 16g protein

Mushroom Soup

Ingredients for each mini baker

2/3 c	(160 ml)	mushrooms, sliced
½ c	(120 ml)	lean beef, sliced thinly
½ c	(120 ml)	onion, chopped fine
2 t	(10 ml)	butter
2 T	(30 ml)	flour
½ c	(60 ml)	milk
½ t	(2 ml)	paprika
¼ t	(1 ml)	dill weed
		salt & pepper to taste

Instructions

Preheat oven to 350° F (175° C). Sauteé mushrooms, onion, and beef in the butter until the onion is slightly caramelized, and the beef is browned.

Blend the milk and spices. Stir the flour into the mushroom mixture, and pour the milk mixture over it.

Cover mini bakers tightly with their lids and bake for 30-45 minutes, until bubbly; serve hot with a baguette.

416 cal • 17g fat • 25g carb • 3g fiber • 40g protein

Chicken Tortilla Soup

Ingredients for each mini baker

½ c	(120 ml)	shredded cooked chicken breast
¼ c	(60 ml)	black beans, canned, rinsed
¼ c	(60 ml)	corn, frozen
½ c	(120 ml)	tomatoes & chilis, canned
½ c	(60 ml)	chicken broth
1 t	(5 ml)	chili powder
¼ t	(1 ml)	cumin
2 T	(10 ml)	corn tortilla, sliced into strips

Instructions

Preheat oven to 350° F (175° C).

Mix together in your mini baker all of the ingredients. Cover tightly and bake in the oven for 30 minutes.

Remove from the oven, stir, garnish with fresh cilantro, and serve with a lime wedge and a nice Mexican beer.

395 cal • 5g fat • 51g carb • 11g fiber • 39g protein

Goulash

Ingredients for each mini baker

4 oz	(115 g)	lean beef, sliced thinly
¼ c	(60 ml)	onion, chopped fine
¼ c	(60 ml)	mushrooms, chopped
¼ c	(60 ml)	tomato sauce
1 t	(5 ml)	paprika
		salt & pepper to taste

Hungary is famous for its paprika, and in a goulash this rich-tasting, it's easy to see why. If you have smoked paprika on hand, substitute it for some (or all) of what this recipe calls for.

Instructions

Preheat oven to 350° F (175° C). Sauteé mushrooms, onion, and beef in the butter until the onion is slightly caramelized, and the beef is browned.

Place beef mixture in mini baker, and mix the tomato sauce and spices together. Pour the tomato sauce over the beef mixture.

Cover mini bakers tightly with their lids and bake for 45 minutes; serve hot with a dollop of sour cream, if you like.

256 cal • 8g fat • 9g carb • 3g fiber • 37g protein

Honey Chicken

Ingredients for each mini baker

1	medium	chicken thigh or drumstick
2	whole	cardamom pods
2 T	(30 ml)	honey
	pinch	sesame seeds

Instructions

Preheat oven to 350° F (175° C), and lightly grease each mini baker.

Place the chicken thigh or drumstick into the mini baker with the cardamom pods, and drizzle the honey over it.

Bake for 45 minutes to an hour, until the juices run clear when you cut into the chicken.

Serve with couscous or rice, and green beans.

418 cal • 11g fat • 37g carb • 1g fiber • 43g protein

Shepherd's Pie

Ingredients for each mini baker

¼ lb	(115 g)	ground beef
2 T	(30 ml)	onion, chopped
¼ c	(60 ml)	frozen corn
1 c	(225 ml)	prepared mashed potatoes, hot*

* You can get away with instant mashed potatoes, following the package directions, but you may prefer to make it from scratch, in which case you'll need:

1	medium	potato, peeled and cubed
2 T	(30 ml)	milk
2 t	(10 ml)	butter

Instructions

Put the ground beef and onion in a skillet, and stir over medium-high heat. Once the onions are soft and the beef is browned, drain if necessary, and add salt and pepper to taste.

Transfer meat mixture to the mini baker and add corn, then spread mashed potatoes* over it. You may find that adding a bit of extra milk makes it easier to spread the potatoes.

Broil under high heat in the oven until the peaks of the potatoes are browned, and serve immediately with a good dark beer.

*If you're making the mashed potatoes from scratch, boil the cubed potato while the beef is browning; once it's fork-tender, drain it and add the milk and butter, mashing into the potatoes with a fork or potato masher.

450 cal • 10g fat • 49g carb • 1g fiber • 41g protein

Scallop Casserole

Ingredients for each mini baker

2 t	(10 ml)	butter
¼ c	(60 ml)	celery, chopped fine
¼ c	(60 ml)	bell pepper, diced
¼ c	(60 ml)	onion, chopped
¼ c	(60 ml)	mushrooms, sliced
1 T	(15 ml)	flour
	pinch	white pepper
	pinch	salt
½ c	(120 ml)	milk
4 oz	(115 g)	bay scallops
¼ c	(60 ml)	breadcrumbs
1 t	(5 ml)	butter, melted
1 T	(15 ml)	cheddar cheese, shredded

Instructions

Preheat oven to 350° F (175° C).

In a small saucepan over medium heat, sauteé celery, bell pepper, onion, and mushrooms in the butter until softened. Stir in flour, salt, and pepper, then gradually add the milk, stirring constantly.

Bring to a boil, then cook and stir for another 2 minutes, or until thickened.

Reduce the heat, and add the scallops. Cook, stirring occasionally, for about 3-4 minutes, or until the scallops are firm and opaque.

Transfer to mini baker, blend breadcrumbs and butter, and sprinkle over the scallop mixture.

Bake for 15-20 minutes, or until bubbly. Top with cheese and return to the oven for another 5 minutes, or until the cheese is melted. Serve hot with a good pinot gris.

465 cal • 19g fat • 42g carb • 3g fiber • 31g protein

Beef Stew

Ingredients for each mini baker

½ c	(120 ml)	potato, peeled and chopped
¼ c	(60 ml)	carrots, peeled and chopped
½ c	(120 ml)	onion, diced
1 t	(5 ml)	olive oil
½ c	(120 ml)	beef, cubed
2 T	(30 ml)	flour
¼ t	(1 ml)	salt
¼ t	(1 ml)	pepper
½ c	(120 ml)	beef broth or bouillon

What could be more perfect than beef stew for dinner? A quick and easy version that you can just as easily throw together for yourself or a crowd.

Instructions

Preheat oven to 325° F (165° C). Chop carrots and potatoes and place in bottom of mini baker. Start onions sautéeing in olive oil over medium-low heat.

Mix flour, salt, and pepper in a bag, and add meat, shaking until it's covered.

Remove the meat from the bag and add it to the onions, continuing to sauteé until the onions are soft and the meat is browned.

Add meat mixture to the vegetables in the mini bakers, and pour broth over it. Cover tightly with mini baker lid, and bake for about an hour, until all is tender. Serve with a good crusty bread and red wine.

379 cal • 12g fat • 30g carb • 4g fiber • 36g protein

Reuben Casserole

Ingredients for each mini baker

½ t	(2 ml)	olive oil
¼ c	(60 ml)	onion, chopped
¼ c	(60 ml)	bell pepper, chopped
½ c	(120 ml)	roast beef or corned beef, cubed
3 oz	(80 g)	sauerkraut, rinsed and drained
¼ c	(60 ml)	condensed cream of chicken soup
¼ c	(60 ml)	Swiss cheese, shredded
1 T	(15 ml)	milk
2 T	(30 ml)	Thousand Island salad dressing
½	slice	rye bread, cubed
1 T	(15 ml)	Swiss cheese, shredded

Instructions

Preheat oven to 350° F (175° C), and grease your mini baker.

Sautée onion and bell pepper in olive oil. Add the beef, sauerkraut, condensed soup, the first ¼ c of cheese, milk, and salad dressing. Stir until warmed through, and transfer to the mini baker.

Arrange the bread cubes over the top, and bake for 15 minutes. Sprinkle with the remaining cheese, and bake for an additional 5-10 minutes, or until the cheese is melted. Serve warm with a cold German beer.

582 cal • 37g fat • 23g carb • 5g fiber • 39g protein

Vegetable Chili

Ingredients for each mini baker

½ t	(2 ml)	oil
2 T	(30 ml)	onion, diced
2 T	(30 ml)	carrot, diced
2 T	(30 ml)	bell pepper, diced
2 T	(30 ml)	celery, diced
1 t	(5 ml)	garlic, diced
¼ c	(60 ml)	beef or vegetable broth
½ t	(2 ml)	chili powder
¼ c	(60 ml)	diced tomatoes, canned
¼ c	(60 ml)	kidney beans, canned
¼ c	(60 ml)	corn, frozen
¼ t	(1 ml)	ground cumin

Instructions

Preheat oven to 350° F (175° C).

Mix all ingredients together in your mini baker. Cover tightly with its lid and place in a shallow baking dish to catch any spills.

Bake for 45 minutes, and serve with fresh cornbread.

263 cal • 3g fat • 46g carb • 11g fiber • 15g protein

Mini Meatloaf

Ingredients for each mini baker

¼ lb	(115 g)	ground beef
1	large	egg
¼ c	(60 ml)	onion, minced
¼ c	(60 ml)	mushrooms, chopped
1/3 c	(75 ml)	breadcrumbs
1 t	(5 ml)	garlic, minced
1 T	(15 ml)	catsup or barbecue sauce
1 t	(5 ml)	Worcestershire sauce
1 t	(5 ml)	brown sugar
1	slice	bacon, cut in half

Instructions

Preheat oven to 350° F (175° C).

Mix all ingredients except the bacon together, blending thoroughly with your hands.

Transfer to your mini baker and cross the pieces of bacon atop the meat, tucking the ends inside the baker. Place the mini baker into a shallow baking dish to catch any spills, cover the mini baker with its lid, and bake for 30 minutes.

Remove the lid and bake for another 15 minutes, or until no longer pink in the center. If you prefer crisp bacon, turn the broiler on for a few minutes at the end, and watch it carefully to avoid burning.

Serve hot with mashed potatoes.

510 cal • 17g fat • 38g carb • 3g fiber • 49g protein

Macaroni & Cheese

Ingredients for each mini baker

¾ c	(180 ml)	milk
2 T	(30 ml)	flour
¾ c	(180 ml)	cheddar cheese, shredded
¼ t	(1 ml)	white pepper
½ c	(120 ml)	macaroni, uncooked
¼ c	(60 ml)	breadcrumbs

Instructions

Preheat oven to 325° F (165° C). Grease your mini baker.

Cook the macaroni just to the al dente stage, drain it, and place it in your mini baker.

Meanwhile, whisk together the milk, flour, and white pepper, then bring to a boil over medium heat (to avoid scorching). Add cheese, stirring constantly until incorporated.

Pour cheese sauce over the macaroni, top with the breadcrumbs, and bake for 30-45 minutes, until the top is browned.

Be sure to let this cool enough before serving it to the kids—it will hold heat for a remarkably long time. Serve with a cold glass of milk.

764 cal • 35g fat • 74g carb • 3g fiber • 38g protein

Index

A

Apple Bran Muffin 22

B

Bacon, Egg & Cheddar Bake 18
Bacon & Shallots Dip 40
Beef Stew 49
Blackberry Cobbler 9
Blueberry Crumble 10
Blueberry Muffin 21
Breakfast Casserole 19
Buffalo Chicken Dip 37

C

Cake, Chocolate Lava 8
Cake, Coffee 26
Candied Sweet Potatoes 34
Cannoli Dip 14
Caprese Baked Eggs 17
Caramel Custard 4
Casserole, Breakfast 19
Casserole, Reuben 50
Casserole, Scallop 48
Cheesy Broccoli 31
Cheesy Garlic Mashed Potatoes ... 35
Chicken, Honey 46
Chicken Tortilla Soup 44
Chili, Vegetable 51
Chocolate Chip Cookie 12
Chocolate Lava Cake 8
Chocolate Pots de Crème 2
Cobbler, Blackberry 9
Coffee Cake 26
Cookie, Chocolate Chip 12

Cup, French Toast 24
Cup, Spanish Egg 16
Custard, Caramel 4
Custard, Pumpkin 3

D

Dip, Bacon & Shallots 40
Dip, Buffalo Chicken 37
Dip, Cannoli 14
Dip, Real Queso Salsa 38
Dip, Sweet Onion 39
Dirty Rice 36

E

Egg & Cheddar Bake 18

F

French Onion Soup 42
French Toast Cup 24

G

German Pancake 25
Gingerbread Soufflé 7
Goulash 45

H

Ham & Spinach Pasta 30
Honey Chicken 46

L

Lemon Poppyseed Muffin 23
Lemon Puff Pudding 5

M

Macaroni & Cheese 53
Mini Meatloaf 52
Monkey Bread 13
Muffin, Apple Bran 22
Muffin, Blueberry 21
Muffin, Lemon Poppyseed 23
Mushroom Soup 43

O

Oats, Scottish 20
Oven Pancake 27

P

Pancake, German 25
Pancake, Oven 27
Paprika Cauliflower 32
Potatoes, Scalloped 33
Pudding, Lemon Puff 5
Pumpkin Custard 3
Pumpkin-Pear Crisp 11

Q

Quiche Lorraine 28

R

Real Queso Salsa Dip 38
Reuben Casserole 50

S

Scallop Casserole 48
Scalloped Potatoes 33
Scottish Oats 20

Shepherd's Pie 47
Soufflé, Gingerbread 7
Soufflé, Yogurt 6
Soup, Chicken Tortilla 44
Soup, French Onion 42
Soup, Mushroom 43
Spanish Egg Cup 16
Sweet Onion Dip 39

V

Vegetable Chili 51

Y

Yogurt Soufflé 6